HELEN KELLER
the world in her heart

by **Lesa Cline-Ransome**

Illustrated by **James Ransome**

Collins
An Imprint of HarperCollinsPublishers

It was March in Alabama, and the warm spring air slipped through the open windows and mingled with the scent of sugar and vanilla. Helen longed to go outside and run barefoot through the still damp grass or climb the tall oak out in front, but the promise of the first bite of her favorite cake kept her inside close to the stove.

Into the kitchen came Viney, the family cook, with a long, sure stride.

She's sure in a hurry.

Viney could tell the cake was just about done and she'd need to test it. Behind her came the light, quick steps of Viney's daughter and Helen's friend, Martha. Martha plopped down, slid close to Helen, and squeezed her hand.

Here comes the cake. Coming out of the oven now.

Heat steamed Helen's face as Viney set the cake, with its burnt vanilla scent, on the table in front of them.

Perfect.

Heels click-clacked across the room and then came the soft scent of lavender.

Mother.

The tender warmth of her mother's lips on Helen's forehead followed. A skirt of silk brushed Helen's arm.

Why is Mother wearing her fancy dress today?
Are we having visitors?

Helen gently petted her dog, Belle, on the back. She felt Belle's body tense and her fur rise and fall. Helen smiled.

The horses are outside.

She felt a door slam and the scrape of boots.

Pa is home early today.

And then she sensed the rumble of an approaching train. . . .

Once, the world had been filled with the sound of her mother's lullabies, the feel of lush green lawn on bare toes, and the sight of gardens overflowing with colorful blossoms. She still enjoyed the soft scent of honeysuckle and the tangy sweetness of the season's first berries, but Helen's world was now silent and dark.

Just before her second birthday, an illness took away her sight and hearing forever. Helen used her hands to feel the mouths of her parents when they spoke and laughed, but she couldn't join in. On rides in the carriage, she could feel the wind blow against her face and the jostle of the bumps along the road, but she couldn't see where they were going.

Helen found ways to speak to her family. For Father, she made the shape of glasses with her fingers. For baby sister Mildred, she sucked her thumb, and for Mother, she laid her hand against her face. But each day she grew more frustrated and angry, hitting Mildred, kicking at her family, and crying. Her parents tried to make her happy, but Helen's behavior only got worse.

They needed help, so they sent for a teacher from the Perkins Institute for the Blind, a school in Boston.

A stranger was here. Helen reached forward to touch her.

A smooth, round face with no lines.

Young.

Curly hair, pulled back smooth.

Neat.

Tight lips, turned up just a little on each end.

Trying to hide a smile.

And her eyes.

Hidden behind glasses.

The stranger will not leave. Each day there is something new. The stranger's hand in hers. Fingers tracing, fists pounding, so many unfamiliar shapes.

What do they mean?

The stranger stayed by her side every minute of the day. Helen tried to hide, but she was always found. She even tried locking the stranger in her room. Nothing worked. Helen reached for her favorite things: her doll, a piece of hard candy, a bowl of cake batter. The stranger always took Helen's hand in hers, fingers tracing, fists pounding, too many strange shapes.

I don't like her.

Helen fought. She cried. She touched her cheek.

I want my mother.

Helen learned her first word at the pump. A cool splash, slippery and wet. *Water*. She learned quickly. With the stranger's help she discovered that each of the movements in her hand was the shape of a letter. And that all of the letters put together made words.

One by one the words came. Perched high in her favorite oak amid the caresses of plants came *tree*. And *leaves*. A smooth, hard something nestled in the palm of her hand. *Egg*. Then *birds* and *nests*.

Helen touched everything in her path. *Tell me the name,* she gestured.

And the stranger taught her to spell the names of her family: *M-o-t-h-e-r;* all the foods she ate: *e-g-g-s* and *b-r-e-a-d* and, her favorite, *c-a-k-e.*

Is there a name for everything?

Y-e-s, the stranger responded.

But who are you? Helen asked by pointing and placing a hand on the stranger's chest.

The letters were spelled slowly into her hand. *T-e-a-c-h-e-r.*

T-e-a-c-h-e-r, Helen spelled back.

I like her.

Soon Helen could spell nearly six hundred words. Stepping onto a well-worn path, leading Teacher down past the old barn, Helen paid close attention. She felt the sharp crunch of pine needles underfoot, then the spongy cushion of moss, and the rickety planks of a bridge.

Almost there, she signaled to Teacher.

When she caught the scent of water she stopped.

W-a-t-e-r, she spelled in Teacher's hand.

T-e-n-n-e-s-s-e-e R-i-v-e-r, Teacher corrected.

Helen dug in mud up to her elbows, filling holes with water, stacking pebbles one by one, and shaping mounds of mud. She trudged home with dirt-caked fingernails and a dress stiff with dirt, but in her head were many new words, such as *o-c-e-a-n*, *d-a-m*, *m-o-u-n-t-a-i-n*, and *v-a-l-l-e-y*.

In the heat of the day, Helen soaked in the warmth as *s-u-n*, *s-k-y*, *p-l-a-n-e-t*, and *s-t-a-r* were traced in her palm.

On other days, as drops poured down on her face, Helen stood perfectly still, her feet in a puddle, drinking in the rain. C-l-o-u-d-s and t-h-u-n-d-e-r she practiced spelling.

But it was in the family garden, fragrant with perfumed blossoms, that Helen discovered her favorite spot. *C-l-e-m-a-t-i-s, l-i-l-y, r-o-s-e*, she spelled as she touched each petal. Surrounded by butterflies and bees, beetles and dragonflies, she felt them whir and crawl and land softly all around her.

With so many new words came many new questions.

Where does the sun go at night? What makes flowers smell so pretty? Why doesn't Belle answer when I spell into her paw?

The words and questions became stories. In her hand, Teacher spelled stories of faraway places from times before Helen was born and read from books that kept Helen awake, wondering, long after her mother had tucked her into bed.

I love Helen, Teacher spelled one morning as they started on their walk.

Helen stopped to respond.

What is love? Helen spelled.

Love is here, Teacher wrote as she held Helen's hand to her heart.

Helen looked confused, so Teacher tried to explain. *Love is . . . ,* she began.

No, she corrected, swiping across Helen's palm with her hand.

She started again.

You cannot touch love, but you can feel the sweetness that it pours into everything. Without love you would not be happy or want to play.

Is that love? Helen asked as she pointed to the sun, with its warmth shining down on the day.

Love is here, Teacher wrote as she held Helen's hand to her heart.

As they continued their walk, Helen thought of their time together, the walks in the woods and gardens, all of the words she could now share with her family. She stopped and placed Annie's hand on her chest.

H-e-l-e-n l-o-v-e-s T-e-a-c-h-e-r, she spelled. When Helen reached to Annie to touch her smooth, round face, all she could feel was a smile that seemed to stretch from ear to ear.

For all those who persevere in the face of adversity
—L.C.-R.

To my cousin Sherlock (who is also deaf),
for taking me to my first comic-book store and
introducing me to the world of drawing
—J.R.

As a child, I loved the story about how Helen Keller changed from a spirited and unmanageable child to a spirited and well-mannered woman. Most interesting was the battle of wills between Helen and her teacher, Annie Sullivan, and how their contentious relationship eventually bloomed into one of mutual love and respect.

Helen Keller made her way through the world using her acute senses of smell, taste, and touch. Her ability to feel vibrations altered the way I perceived nonhearing people. I especially admired the way in which she "saw" the world through her connection to people, nature, social causes, and writing. In reading and writing about Helen's transformation, I underwent my own in seeing the world through the unseeing eyes of an amazing woman, Helen Keller.—L.C.-R.

Reading about the people I am illustrating is a large part of my research. Helen loved wandering through her family's garden and could distinguish between flowers by using her keen senses of smell and touch. The image of Helen standing in the garden reminded me of one of my favorite paintings, *Carnation, Lily, Lily, Rose* by John Singer Sargent. I often choose an artist or an art style as the muse for my illustrations, and Sargent, who painted in the 1880s, became my inspiration for *Helen Keller*.

When Annie Sullivan arrives at the Keller household, she is wearing sunglasses because her failing eyes were sensitive to sunlight. In my paintings, Annie is shown indoors and outdoors. I used the sunglasses as a visual metaphor; the barrier is removed once Helen and Annie embark on their journey of learning together.—J.R.

Collins is an imprint of HarperCollins Publishers. Helen Keller: The World in Her Heart Text copyright © 2008 by Lesa Cline-Ransome Illustrations copyright © 2008 by James Ransome Manufactured in China. All rights reserved. No part of this book may be used or reproduced in any manner whatsoever without written permission except in the case of brief quotations embodied in critical articles and reviews. For information address HarperCollins Children's Books, a division of HarperCollins Publishers, 1350 Avenue of the Americas, New York, NY 10019. www.harpercollinschildrens.com Library of Congress Cataloging-in-Publication Data Cline-Ransome, Lesa.   Helen Keller : the world in her heart / Lesa Cline-Ransome ; illustrated by James Ransome. — 1st ed.   p.   cm.   ISBN 978-0-06-057074-3 (trade bdg.) — ISBN 978-0-06-057075-0 (lib. bdg.) 1. Keller, Helen, 1880-1968—Juvenile literature. 2. Deaf and blind women—United States—Biography—Juvenile literature. 3. Deaf and blind people—United States—Biography—Juvenile literature. I. Ransome, James, ill. II. Title. HV1624.K4C65 2008   2007025851   362.4'1092—dc22   [B] Designed by Stephanie Bart-Horvath 1 2 3 4 5 6 7 8 9 10 ❖ First Edition